STEP-BY-STEP

Cooking for One & Two

STEP-BY-STEP

Cooking for One & Two

ROSEMARY WADEY

PARRAGON

First published in Great Britain in 1995 by
Parragon Book Service Ltd
Unit 13–17
Avonbridge Trading Estate
Atlantic Road
Avonmouth
Bristol BS11 9QD

ISBN 1-85813-940-6 (hbk)
ISBN 0-75251-257-9 (pbk)

Produced by Haldane Mason, London

Printed in Italy

Acknowledgements:
Art Direction: Ron Samuels
Editor: Joanna Swinnerton
Series Design: Pedro & Frances Prá-Lopez/Kingfisher Design
Page Design: Somewhere Creative
Photography: Joff Lee
Styling: John Lee Studios
Home Economist: Rosemary Wadey

Photographs on pages 6, 18, 34, 48 and 62 are reproduced by permission of ZEFA Picture Library UK Ltd.

Note:
Cup measurements in this book are for American cups. Tablespoons are assumed to be 15 ml. Unless otherwise stated, milk is assumed to be full-fat, eggs are standard size 2 and pepper is freshly ground black pepper.

Contents

SOUPS & STARTERS *page 7*

Chicken & Sweetcorn Chowder 8
Leek, Potato & Carrot Soup 10
Smoked Salmon Pâté with Avocado 12
Peppered Camembert & Nectarine Salad 14
Walnut, Egg & Cheese Pâté 16

SNACKS & QUICK MEALS *page 19*

Spinach Filo Baskets 20
Courgette (Zucchini), Tarragon & Bacon Quiches 22
Sweetcorn & Potato Fritters 24
Chicken & Almond Rissoles with Stir-fried Vegetables 27
Macaroni & Tuna Fish Layer 28
Aubergine (Eggplant) with Risotto Stuffing 30
Broccoli with Fluffy Eggs 32

TWO-DAY MEALS & SNACKS *page 35*

Salmon with Avocado & Tarragon Sauce/Kedgeree 36
Pasta Medley 38
Crunchy-topped Chicken/Spiced Chicken Salad 40
Italian Tomato Sauce with Pasta/Ocean Pie 43
Tabbouleh Salad 44
Bobotie/Creamy Curried Beef 46

MAIN COURSES *page 49*

Seafish Bundles 50
Scallop & Bacon Kebab 52
Coq au Vin Blanc 55
Pan-fried Liver with Thyme & Capers 56
Noisettes of Lamb with Spicy Sauce 58
Turkish Lamb Stew 60

DESSERTS *page 63*

Lime Cheesecakes 64
Ginger & Apricot Alaskas 66
Raspberry & Orange Pancake Bundles 68
Pink Syllabubs 71
Rice & Banana Brûlée 72
White Chocolate Pots 74

MEALS FOR ONE & TWO *page 76*

Index 80

CHAPTER ONE

Soups & Starters

Soups and starters can easily be served as light meals and snacks too, a very important part of cooking for only one or two people. But having said that, it is essential that you always prepare, cook and serve proper meals, whether you are on your own, in a twosome or part of a large family; these soups and starters are filling, nutritious and easy to make. The soups in particular can be made in large quantities to serve over two or three days, or frozen for future use, which will save you from spending too much time in the kitchen.

When it comes to planning an elegant meal for two, the recipes here cover a wide range of tastes and suggest slightly different ways of serving old favourites. Soups are always popular; the blend of nectarines with peppered Camembert conjures up a new taste; smoked salmon pâté complements an avocado beautifully; and a vegetarian cheese pâté will suit all tastes.

Opposite: *A simple soup makes an excellent meal for one or two people; it is easy to prepare and satisfying to eat.*

STEP 1

STEP 2

STEP 3

STEP 4

CHICKEN & SWEETCORN CHOWDER

A quick and satisfying soup, full of flavour and different textures. This will serve two people for one day or one person for two days.

SERVES 2

2 tsp oil
15 g/½ oz/1 tbsp butter or margarine
1 small onion, chopped finely
1 chicken leg quarter or 2–3 drumsticks
1 tbsp plain (all-purpose) flour
600 ml/1 pint/2½ cups chicken stock
½ small red, yellow or orange (bell) pepper, seeded and chopped finely
2 large tomatoes, peeled and chopped
2 tsp tomato purée (paste)
200 g/7 oz can of sweetcorn, drained
generous pinch of dried oregano
¼ tsp ground coriander
salt and pepper
chopped fresh parsley to garnish

1 Heat the oil and butter or margarine in a saucepan and fry the onion gently until beginning to soften. Cut the chicken quarter, if using, into 2 pieces. Add the chicken to the saucepan and fry until golden brown all over.

2 Add the flour and cook for 1–2 minutes. Then add the stock gradually, bring to the boil and simmer for 5 minutes.

3 Add the (bell) pepper, tomatoes, tomato purée (paste), sweetcorn, oregano, coriander and seasoning. Cover and simmer gently for about 20 minutes until the chicken is very tender.

4 Remove the chicken from the soup, strip off the flesh and chop finely. Return the chopped meat to the soup.

5 Adjust the seasoning and simmer for a further 2–3 minutes before sprinkling with parsley and serving very hot with crusty bread.

CHICKEN

If preferred, the chicken may be removed from the soup when tender to serve separately.

STEP 1

STEP 2

STEP 4

STEP 5

LEEK, POTATO & CARROT SOUP

A quick chunky soup, ideal for a snack or a quick lunch. The leftovers can be puréed to make one portion of creamed soup for the next day.

SERVES 2

1 leek, about 175 g/6 oz
1 tbsp oil
1 garlic clove, crushed
750 ml/1¼ pints/3 cups chicken or vegetable stock
1 bay leaf
¼ tsp ground cumin
175 g/6 oz/1 cup potatoes, diced
125 g/4 oz/1 cup carrot, grated coarsely
salt and pepper
chopped fresh parsley to garnish

PUREED SOUP:
5–6 tbsp milk
1–2 tbsp double (heavy) cream, crème fraîche or soured cream

1 Trim off some of the coarse green part of the leek, then slice thinly and rinse in cold water. Drain well.

2 Heat the oil in a saucepan, add the leek and garlic, and fry gently for 2–3 minutes until soft but barely coloured. Add the stock, bay leaf, cumin and seasoning, and bring to the boil.

3 Add the diced potato to the saucepan, cover and simmer gently for 10–15 minutes until the potato is just tender but not broken up.

4 Add the grated carrot and simmer for a further 2–3 minutes. Adjust the seasoning, discard the bay leaf and serve sprinkled liberally with chopped parsley.

5 To make a puréed soup, first purée the leftovers (about half the original soup) in a blender or food processor or press through a sieve (strainer) until smooth and then return to a clean saucepan with the milk. Bring to the boil and simmer for 2–3 minutes. Adjust the seasoning and stir in the cream or crème fraîche before serving sprinkled with chopped parsley.

HELPFUL HINT

If you make double quantities of this soup, half can be frozen to use at a later date.

SMOKED SALMON PATE WITH AVOCADO

Use trimmings of smoked salmon blended with hard-boiled (hard-cooked) egg and soft cheese to serve garnished with slices of avocado and tomatoes for an elegant starter for two or main dish for one.

STEP 1

STEP 3

STEP 5

STEP 6

SERVES 1–2

60 g/2 oz smoked salmon pieces
1 hard-boiled (hard-cooked) egg
45 g/1½ oz/3 tbsp low-fat soft cheese
1 small garlic clove, crushed (optional)
1 tsp lemon or lime juice
about 2 tbsp natural fromage frais or natural yogurt
1–2 tomatoes
1 ripe avocado
1 tbsp French dressing
pepper
watercress to garnish

1 Put the pieces of smoked salmon into a food processor and process until finely chopped. Alternatively, chop the smoked salmon very finely.

2 Add the hard-boiled (hard-cooked) egg and continue processing until well chopped and blended, then add the soft cheese, garlic, lemon or lime juice and pepper. Continue processing until well blended. Alternatively, grate the egg finely into the other ingredients and mix.

3 Add sufficient fromage frais or yogurt to give a piping consistency and place in a piping bag fitted with a large star nozzle (tip). Chill until needed.

4 Halve the tomatoes and cut into thin wedges. Halve the avocado, peel carefully and remove the stone (pit). Cut each avocado half into a fan by slicing from the round end to the narrow stem end but leaving a 'hinge'.

5 Spread out the avocado fan on a small plate, interleaving the tomato wedges with the avocado slices.

6 Pipe or spoon a whirl of smoked salmon pâté at the stem end of the avocado fan.

7 Spoon a little French dressing over each tomato and avocado fan, garnish with watercress and serve with crackers, toast or crusty bread.

VARIATIONS

Smoked mackerel or kippers may be used for the pâté instead of smoked salmon. The pâté may also be piped to fill the cavities of avocado halves.

STEP 1

STEP 2

STEP 3

STEP 5

PEPPERED CAMEMBERT & NECTARINE SALAD

An unusual blend of flavours and textures, but one that certainly whets the appetite.

SERVES 1

1–2 × 30 g/1 oz portions Camembert cheese
1 tbsp coarse steak pepper
1–2 nectarines
4 cm / 1½ inch piece cucumber
15 g /½ oz pecan halves or cashew nuts
mixed lettuce leaves (salad greens)

DRESSING:
1 tbsp sesame oil
1 tsp balsamic vinegar
generous pinch of dry mustard
pinch of sugar
1 garlic clove, crushed (optional)
salt and pepper

1 Cut the rind off the Camembert cheese. Cut the cheese into cubes or slices and roll in the coarse pepper. Chill.

2 Halve the nectarines, remove the stone (pit) and slice thinly. Put into a bowl.

3 Cut the cucumber into dice or thin narrow sticks and add to the nectarines with the nuts.

4 Whisk all the ingredients for the dressing together, adding seasoning to taste, and pour over the nectarine salad; toss lightly.

5 Arrange a few mixed lettuce leaves (salad greens) on a serving plate and spoon the salad on top.

6 Arrange the peppered Camembert on the salad and serve with crusty bread or rolls.

VARIATIONS

Brie may be used instead of Camembert, and peaches can be used in place of the nectarines, if you prefer.

STEP 1

STEP 2

STEP 3

STEP 4

WALNUT, EGG & CHEESE PATE

This unusual mixture, flavoured with parsley and dill, can be served as a pâté with crackers, crusty bread or toast, or used as a stuffing for tomatoes, celery or other vegetables.

SERVES 2

1 celery stick
1–2 spring onions (scallions), trimmed
30 g/1 oz/¼ cup shelled walnuts
1 tbsp chopped fresh parsley
1 tsp chopped fresh dill or ½ tsp dried dillweed
1 garlic clove, crushed
generous dash Worcestershire sauce
125 g/4 oz/½ cup cottage cheese
60 g/2 oz/½ cup blue cheese, such as Stilton or Danish Blue
1 hard-boiled (hard-cooked) egg
30 g/1 oz/2 tbsp butter
salt and pepper
fresh herbs to garnish

1 Chop the celery finely, slice the spring onions (scallions) very finely and chop the walnuts evenly but not too finely. Place in a bowl.

2 Add the chopped herbs, garlic, and Worcestershire sauce, and mix well, then stir the cottage cheese evenly through the mixture.

3 Grate the blue cheese and hard-boiled (hard-cooked) egg finely into the pâté mixture, and season to taste.

4 Melt the butter and stir through the pâté, then spoon into one serving dish or two individual dishes, but do not press down firmly. Chill until set.

5 Garnish with fresh herbs and serve with crackers, toast or fresh, crusty bread, and a few crudités, if liked.

STUFFING

To use as a stuffing, cut the tops off extra-large tomatoes, scoop out the seeds and fill with the pâté, piling it well up, or spoon into the hollows of celery sticks cut into 5 cm/2 inch pieces.

REAL ENGLISH CUTLERY
SHEFFIELD
MADE
STAINLESS

CHAPTER TWO

Snacks & Quick Meals

Being able to prepare food quickly can be very important in our busy lives, as we often need a quick meal or snack during the day or before going out, but have limited time in which to make it. No one wants to spend too much time in the kitchen, so the following recipes have been devised with speed in mind, and they cater for all tastes and times of day as well as for individuals and couples.

With a little imagination, a quick meal can be just as satisfying as any other meal. A pasta and tuna fish layer can be varied by using cooked chicken or other cold meats, or vegetables in a savoury sauce; quiches are just as good hot as cold; rissoles can use up any type of cooked meat for a really tasty snack with a mixture of stir-fried vegetables; and sweetcorn and potato fritters double up well for breakfast (perhaps with bacon or sausages), brunch or an anytime snack.

Opposite: *Dried pasta is a particularly useful ingredient for meals for one or two. It will keep in your store cupboard for a considerable time, can be bought in a wide variety of shapes and flavours, and is quick and easy to cook.*

STEP 2

STEP 4

STEP 5

STEP 6

SPINACH FILO BASKETS

If you use frozen spinach, it only needs to be defrosted and drained before being mixed with the cheeses and seasonings. Filo pastry can be defrosted sufficiently to remove the four sheets of pastry you need, then returned to the freezer to use at a later date.

MAKES 2

125 g/4 oz/3 cups fresh leaf spinach, washed and chopped roughly, or 90 g/ 3 oz/1/2 cup defrosted frozen spinach
2–4 spring onions (scallions), trimmed and chopped, or 1 tbsp finely chopped onion
1 garlic clove, crushed
2 tbsp grated Parmesan cheese
90 g/3 oz/3/4 cup mature (sharp) Cheddar cheese, grated
large pinch of ground allspice
1 egg yolk
4 sheets filo pastry
30 g/1 oz/2 tbsp butter, melted
salt and pepper
2 spring onions (scallions) to garnish

1 If using fresh spinach, cook it in the minimum of boiling salted water for 3–4 minutes until tender. Drain very thoroughly, using a potato masher to remove excess liquid, then chop and put into a bowl. If using frozen spinach, simply drain and chop.

2 Add the spring onions (scallions) or onion, garlic, cheeses, allspice, egg yolk and seasoning, and mix well.

3 Grease 2 individual Yorkshire pudding tins (muffin pans), or ovenproof dishes or tins (pans) about 12 cm/5 inches in diameter, and 4 cm/ 1 1/2 inches deep. Cut the filo pastry sheets in half to make 8 pieces and brush each lightly with melted butter.

4 Place one piece of filo pastry in a tin (pan) or dish and then cover with a second piece at right angles to the first. Add two more pieces at right angles, so that all the corners are in different places. Line the other tin (pan) in the same way.

5 Spoon the spinach mixture into the 'baskets' and place in a preheated oven at 180°C/350°F/Gas Mark 4 for about 20 minutes, or until the pastry is golden brown. Garnish with a spring onion (scallion) tassel and serve hot or cold.

6 Make spring onion (scallion) tassels about 30 minutes before required. Trim off the root end and cut to a length of 5–7 cm/2–3 inches. Make a series of cuts from the green end to within 2 cm/ 3/4 inch of the other end. Place in a bowl of iced water to open out. Drain well before use.

STEP 3

STEP 4

STEP 5

STEP 6

COURGETTE (ZUCCHINI), TARRAGON & BACON QUICHES

Individual pastry cases with a filling of grated courgettes (zucchini), fresh tarragon and crispy bacon in a fromage frais custard to serve hot or cold.

MAKES 2

PASTRY:
90 g/3 oz/¾ cup plain (all-purpose) flour
pinch of salt
45 g/1½ oz/3 tbsp butter or block margarine

FILLING:
1 small courgette (zucchini), about 90 g/3 oz
60 g/2 oz/4 slices lean bacon, derinded and diced
1 spring onion (scallion), trimmed and chopped
¼ tsp chopped fresh tarragon or a generous pinch of dried tarragon
1 egg
6 tbsp natural fromage frais
1–2 tsp grated Parmesan cheese
salt and pepper

1 To make the pastry, sift the flour and salt into a bowl and rub in the butter or margarine until the mixture resembles fine breadcrumbs. Add sufficient cold water to mix to a pliable dough and knead very lightly. Then wrap the pastry in clingfilm (plastic wrap) and chill while preparing the filling.

2 Trim the courgette (zucchini) and grate coarsely into a bowl. Cover with boiling water and leave for 5 minutes; then drain very thoroughly, using a potato masher if necessary to extract the water.

3 Fry the bacon in its own fat until well sealed, then add to the courgette (zucchini) with the spring onion (scallion) and tarragon.

4 Roll out the pastry and use to line 2 individual fluted flan tins (pans) about 11 cm/4½ inches in diameter.

5 Divide the courgette (zucchini) mixture between the 2 tins (pans). Beat the egg with the fromage frais and season well.

6 Pour the custard into the cases, sprinkle with the cheese and place in a preheated oven at 200°C/400°F/Gas Mark 6 for 25–30 minutes, or until the custard is set firm and the pastry is cooked through. Serve hot or cold. The quiches can be frozen for up to 2 months.

STEP 2

STEP 3

STEP 4

STEP 5

SWEETCORN & POTATO FRITTERS

An ideal supper dish for two, or for one if you halve the quantities. You can use the remaining sweetcorn in another recipe.

SERVES 2

2 tbsp oil
1 small onion, sliced thinly
1 garlic clove, crushed
350 g/12 oz potatoes
200 g/7 oz can of sweetcorn, drained
½ tsp dried oregano
1 egg, beaten
60 g/2 oz/½ cup Edam or Gouda cheese, grated
salt and pepper
2–4 eggs
2–4 tomatoes, sliced
parsley sprigs, to garnish

1 Heat 1 tablespoon of the oil in a non-stick frying pan (skillet). Add the onion and garlic, and fry very gently until soft, but only lightly coloured, stirring frequently. Remove from the heat.

2 Grate the potatoes coarsely into a bowl and mix in the sweetcorn, oregano, beaten egg and seasoning; then add the fried onion.

3 Heat the remaining oil in the frying pan (skillet). Divide the potato mixture in half and add to the pan to make 2 oval-shaped cakes, levelling and shaping the cakes with a palette knife (spatula).

4 Cook gently for about 10 minutes until browned underneath and almost cooked through, keeping in shape with the palette knife (spatula) and loosening so they don't stick.

5 Sprinkle each potato fritter with the grated cheese and place under a preheated moderately hot grill (broiler) until golden brown.

6 Meanwhile, poach either 1 or 2 eggs for each person until just cooked. Transfer the fritters to warmed plates and top each with the eggs and sliced tomatoes. Garnish with parsley and serve at once.

CHICKEN & ALMOND RISSOLES WITH STIR-FRIED VEGETABLES

Cooked potatoes and cooked chicken are combined to make tasty rissoles rolled in chopped almonds to serve with stir-fried vegetables.

SERVES 1

125 g/4 oz boiled potatoes
90 g/3 oz carrots
125 g/4 oz/1 cup cooked chicken meat
1 garlic clove, crushed
½ tsp dried tarragon or thyme
generous pinch of ground allspice or coriander
1 egg yolk, or ½ egg, beaten
about 30 g/1 oz/¼ cup flaked (slivered) almonds
salt and pepper

STIR-FRIED VEGETABLES:
1 celery stick
2 spring onions (scallions), trimmed
1 tbsp oil
8 baby sweetcorn cobs
about 10–12 mangetouts (snow peas) or sugar snap peas, trimmed
2 tsp balsamic vinegar

1 Grate the boiled potatoes and raw carrots coarsely into a bowl. Chop finely or mince (grind) the chicken and add to the vegetables with the garlic, tarragon, allspice or coriander and plenty of seasoning.

2 Add the egg yolk or beaten egg and bind the ingredients together.

3 Divide the mixture in half and shape each into a sausage.

4 Chop the almonds evenly and then roll each rissole in the nuts until evenly coated. Either place in a greased ovenproof dish and cook in a preheated oven at 200°C/400°F/Gas Mark 6 for about 20 minutes, or until lightly browned; or fry in a little oil until browned all over and cooked through.

5 While the rissoles cook, prepare the stir-fried vegetables. Cut the celery and spring onions (scallions) into narrow slanting slices. Heat the oil in a frying pan (skillet) and toss in these vegetables. Cook over a high heat for 1–2 minutes, then add the sweetcorn cobs and peas and cook for 2–3 minutes. Finally, add the vinegar and seasoning to taste.

6 Spoon the stir-fried vegetables on to a serving plate and place the rissoles beside them. Serve at once.

LEFTOVERS

Any leftover cooked meat or poultry can be used for this dish.

STEP 1

STEP 3

STEP 4

STEP 5

STEP 2

STEP 3

STEP 4

STEP 5

MACARONI & TUNA FISH LAYER

A layer of tuna fish with garlic, mushroom and red (bell) pepper is sandwiched between two layers of macaroni with a crunchy topping.

SERVES 2

125–150 g/4–5 oz/1¼ cup dried macaroni
2 tbsp oil
1 garlic clove, crushed
60 g/2 oz/¾ cup button mushrooms, sliced
½ red (bell) pepper, thinly sliced
200 g/7 oz can of tuna fish in brine, drained and flaked
½ tsp dried oregano
30 g/1 oz/2 tbsp butter or margarine
1 tbsp plain (all-purpose) flour
250 ml/8 fl oz/1 cup milk
2 tomatoes, sliced
2 tbsp dried breadcrumbs
30 g/1 oz/¼ cup mature (sharp) Cheddar or Parmesan cheese, grated
salt and pepper

1 Cook the macaroni in boiling salted water, with 1 tablespoon of the oil added, until tender, about 12 minutes. Drain, rinse and drain thoroughly.

2 Heat the remaining oil in a saucepan or frying pan (skillet) and fry the garlic, mushrooms and (bell) pepper until soft. Add the tuna fish, oregano and seasoning, and heat through.

3 Grease an ovenproof dish (about 1 litre/1¾ pint/4 cup capacity), and add half the cooked macaroni. Cover with the tuna mixture and then add the remaining macaroni.

4 To make the sauce, melt the butter or margarine in a saucepan, stir in the flour and cook for 1 minute. Add the milk gradually and bring to the boil. Simmer for a minute or so, stirring continuously, until thickened. Season to taste. Pour the sauce over the macaroni.

5 Lay the sliced tomatoes over the sauce and sprinkle with the breadcrumbs and cheese.

6 Place in a preheated oven at 200°C/400°F/Gas Mark 6 for about 25 minutes, or until piping hot and the top is well browned.

VARIATIONS

Ring the changes by replacing the tuna fish with chopped cooked chicken, beef, pork or ham or with 3–4 sliced hard-boiled (hard-cooked) eggs.

AUBERGINE (EGGPLANT) WITH RISOTTO STUFFING

An aubergine (eggplant) is halved and filled with a risotto mixture, topped with cheese and baked to make a snack or quick meal for two, or an accompaniment to a main dish.

STEP 2

STEP 3

STEP 5

STEP 6

SERVES 2

60 g/2 oz/¼ cup mixed long-grain and wild rice
1 aubergine (eggplant), about 350 g/12 oz
1 tbsp olive oil
1 small onion, chopped finely
1 garlic clove, crushed
½ small red (bell) pepper, cored, deseeded and chopped
2 tbsp water
30 g/1 oz/3 tbsp raisins
30 g/1 oz/¼ cup cashew nuts, chopped roughly
½ tsp dried oregano
45 g/1½ oz/⅓ cup mature (sharp) Cheddar or Parmesan cheese, grated
salt and pepper
fresh oregano or parsley to garnish

1 Cook the rice in boiling salted water until just tender, about 15 minutes. Drain, rinse and drain again.

2 Bring a large saucepan of water to the boil. Cut the stem off the aubergine (eggplant) and then cut in half lengthwise. Cut out the flesh from the centre carefully, leaving about a 1.5 cm/½ inch shell. Blanch the shells in the boiling water for 3–4 minutes. Drain thoroughly.

3 Chop the aubergine (eggplant) flesh finely. Heat the oil in a saucepan or frying pan (skillet) and fry the onion and garlic gently until beginning to soften, then add the (bell) pepper and aubergine (eggplant) flesh and continue cooking for a couple of minutes before adding the water and cooking for a further 2–3 minutes.

4 Stir the raisins, cashew nuts, oregano and rice into the aubergine (eggplant) mixture and season well with salt and pepper.

5 Lay the aubergine (eggplant) shells in an ovenproof dish and spoon in the rice mixture, piling it up well. Cover and place in a preheated oven at 190°C/375°F/Gas Mark 5 for 20 minutes.

6 Remove the lid and sprinkle the cheese over the rice. Place under a preheated moderate grill (broiler) for 3–4 minutes until golden brown. Serve hot garnished with oregano or parsley.

STEP 3

STEP 4

STEP 5

STEP 6

BROCCOLI WITH FLUFFY EGGS

Broccoli or cauliflower florets in a mustard sauce are topped with an egg yolk set in whisked egg white and finished off with grated cheese.

SERVES 1

175 g/6 oz/1½ cups trimmed broccoli or cauliflower florets
15 g/½ oz/1 tbsp butter or margarine
15 g/½ oz/2 tbsp flour
150 ml/¼ pint/⅔ cup milk
1 tbsp coarse grain mustard
squeeze of lemon juice
90 g/3 oz/¾ cup mature (sharp) Cheddar cheese, grated
1 large egg, separated
salt and pepper
paprika to garnish

1 Cook the broccoli or cauliflower in boiling salted water until tender but still crisp, about 3–4 minutes.

2 Meanwhile, melt the butter or margarine in a small saucepan, stir in the flour and cook for a minute or so. Add the milk gradually, stirring continuously, and bring to the boil until thickened. Season well, stir in the mustard and lemon juice and simmer for 1–2 minutes.

3 Remove the sauce from the heat and stir in two thirds of the cheese until melted.

4 Drain the broccoli or cauliflower very thoroughly and place on an ovenproof plate or dish. Pour the sauce over the vegetables.

5 Whisk the egg white until very stiff and season lightly. Pile the egg white on top of the broccoli or cauliflower and make a well in the centre.

6 Drop the egg yolk into the well in the egg white and sprinkle with the remaining cheese. Place under a preheated moderate grill (broiler) for 3–4 minutes until the meringue is lightly browned and the cheese melted. Serve sprinkled with paprika.

VARIATIONS

The fluffy eggs can be served on a variety of other vegetables with or without a sauce, or on poached haddock.

CHAPTER THREE

Two-day Meals & Snacks

When you are on your own, the task of cooking for just one or two can become a little tedious. Such small quantities usually take less time to prepare, but the cooking time is the same as for several people, so it is often a good idea to cook sufficient for two days. Alternatively, you can cook two portions of the main ingredient, such as chicken pieces or a tomato sauce, and set aside one portion, ready to be turned into a different meal the following day. The recipes in this section are devised with both of these possibilities in mind, including two salads which will improve with keeping overnight in the refrigerator.

For example, if you like salmon, simply poach two portions and serve one with a sauce on one day, and make the other into kedgeree the next; cook a spicy mince and then transform it into a creamy curry to serve with poppadoms and chutney; serve roast chicken thighs with a crunchy topping, then use half of the meat to make a spicy chicken salad, served with rice.

Supermarkets are good at providing single and small portions, particularly of meat and fish. Small fish, chops and cutlets are ideal for meals for one or two. It takes only a little imagination to conjure up lots of new ideas, even if you are cooking small quantities.

Opposite: *Use as wide a range of ingredients as you can, and use the freshest fruits and vegetables available to ensure that your meals are varied and full of flavour.*

STEP 1

STEP 2

STEP 4

STEP 6

SALMON WITH AVOCADO & TARRAGON SAUCE/KEDGEREE

Two salmon cutlets or fillets are cooked at the same time, one to serve with a delicious avocado sauce and the other to be made into a kedgeree the next day.

SERVES 1

2 × 175 g/6 oz salmon cutlets or fillets
butter
1 bay leaf
1 tsp lemon juice
salt and pepper

SAUCE:
½ ripe avocado
1 tsp lemon juice
2 tbsp soured cream or natural fromage frais
1 spring onion (scallion), trimmed and chopped finely, or 1½ tsp chopped chives
1 tsp chopped fresh tarragon or ½ tsp dried

SALMON KEDGEREE:
60 g/2 oz/¼ cup long-grain rice
15 g/½ oz/1 tbsp butter or margarine
1 small onion, sliced thinly
1 garlic clove, crushed
1 tsp chopped fresh tarragon or 2 tsp chopped fresh parsley
1 hard-boiled (hard-cooked) egg, chopped
2 tbsp soured cream or natural fromage frais
salt and pepper

1 Season the salmon. Lightly butter a sheet of foil large enough to enclose the fish, and place the salmon on it. Add the bay leaf and lemon juice, and seal the edges of the parcel of foil firmly.

2 Place the parcel in a saucepan and cover with cold water. Bring to the boil, cover and simmer for 10 minutes. Remove from the heat and leave for 5 minutes. Remove from the pan.

3 To make the sauce, mash the avocado with the lemon juice, then add the soured cream, spring onion (scallion) or chives, tarragon and seasoning, beating until smooth.

4 Remove one salmon piece and place on a plate. Spoon the avocado sauce around the fish and serve. Let the other salmon piece cool, then chill and set aside for the kedgeree.

5 To make the kedgeree, cook the rice in boiling salted water for 12–14 minutes, then drain. Remove the skin and bones from the salmon and flake.

6 Melt the butter or margarine in a saucepan and fry the onion and garlic gently until soft, then add the flaked salmon and cooked rice and heat through completely, stirring almost continuously. Add the tarragon or parsley, chopped egg, soured cream or fromage frais and plenty of seasoning, and heat gently. Serve piping hot.

STEP 1

STEP 2

STEP 3

STEP 4

PASTA MEDLEY

Strips of cooked chicken or pork are tossed with coloured pasta in a pesto-flavoured dressing with grapes and carrot sticks. This will keep well to be eaten again the next day; if you like, throw in a few new ingredients to change the flavour a little.

SERVES 2

125–150 g/4–5 oz dried pasta shapes, such as twists or bows
1 tbsp oil
1 tbsp French dressing
2 tbsp thick mayonnaise
2 tsp bottled pesto sauce
1 tbsp soured cream or natural fromage frais
175 g/6 oz cooked chicken meat or lean cooked pork
1–2 celery sticks
125 g/4 oz/1 cup black grapes (preferably seedless)
1 large carrot, trimmed
salt and pepper
celery leaves to garnish

1 Cook the pasta in boiling salted water with the oil until just tender, about 12 minutes. Drain thoroughly, rinse and drain again. Transfer to a bowl and mix in the French dressing while hot; leave until cold.

2 Combine the mayonnaise, pesto sauce and soured cream or fromage frais in a bowl, and season to taste.

3 Cut the chicken or pork into narrow strips. Cut the celery diagonally into narrow slices. Reserve a few grapes for garnish, halve the rest and remove any pips (seeds). Cut the carrot into narrow julienne strips.

4 Add the chicken or pork, celery, halved grapes, carrot and mayonnaise to the pasta, and toss thoroughly; adjust the seasoning.

5 Arrange the salad on 2 plates and garnish with the remaining grapes and celery leaves.

FRENCH DRESSING

You can make your own French dressing by whisking together 1 part wine vinegar to 3 parts olive oil, and seasoning to taste.

VARIATIONS

Other vegetables and fruit that are available can be used to ring the changes for this salad, but make sure the flavours and textures complement each other.

STEP 1

STEP 2

STEP 4

STEP 5

CRUNCHY-TOPPED CHICKEN/ SPICED CHICKEN SALAD

Cook four chicken pieces together, and serve two hot, topped with a crunchy herb mixture and white sauce, accompanied by potatoes or pasta, then turn the remainder into a spicy chicken salad.

SERVES 2

4 chicken thighs
oil for brushing
garlic powder
½ dessert (eating) apple, grated coarsely
1½ tbsp dry parsley and thyme stuffing mix
salt and pepper

SAUCE:
15 g/½ oz/1 tbsp butter or margarine
2 tsp plain (all-purpose) flour
5 tbsp milk
2 tbsp dry white wine or stock
½ tsp dried mustard powder
1 tsp capers or chopped gherkins

SPICED CHICKEN SALAD:
½ small onion, chopped finely
1 tbsp oil
1 tsp tomato purée (paste)
½ tsp curry powder
1 tsp apricot jam
1 tsp lemon juice
2 tbsp mayonnaise
1 tbsp soured cream or natural fromage frais
90 g/3 oz/¾ cup seedless grapes, halved
60 g/2 oz/¼ cup long-grain rice, cooked

1 Place the chicken in an ovenproof dish. Brush with oil, add garlic powder, and season. Place in a preheated oven at 200°C/400°F/Gas Mark 6 for 25 minutes, or until almost cooked.

2 Mix the apple with the stuffing. Baste the chicken and spoon the mixture over 2 of the pieces. Return to the oven until the mixture is brown and the chicken is cooked, about 10 minutes.

3 To make the sauce, melt the fat in a saucepan, stir in the flour and cook for 1–2 minutes. Add the milk gradually, then the wine or stock, and bring to the boil. Stir in the mustard, capers or gherkins and seasoning, and simmer for a minute or so. Serve the 2 pieces of chicken with the crunchy topping with the sauce spooned over and around it.

4 For the salad, fry the onion gently in the oil until barely coloured. Add the tomato purée (paste), curry powder and jam, and cook for 1 minute. Leave to cool. Blend in a food processor, or press through a sieve (strainer). Beat in the lemon juice, mayonnaise and soured cream or fromage frais. Season.

5 Cut the chicken into strips and add to the sauce with the grapes. Mix well, and chill for at least 2 hours before serving with rice and a green salad.

ITALIAN TOMATO SAUCE WITH PASTA/OCEAN PIE

Fresh tomatoes make a delicious Italian-style sauce which goes equally well with pasta and bacon or white fish and prawns (shrimp) to give two totally different dishes.

SERVES 1

1 tbsp olive oil
1 small onion, chopped finely
1–2 cloves garlic, crushed
350 g/12 oz tomatoes, peeled and chopped
2 tsp tomato purée (paste)
2 tbsp water
75–90 g/2½–3 oz dried pasta shapes
90 g/3 oz/¾ cup lean bacon, derinded and diced
45 g/1½ oz/½ cup mushrooms, sliced
1 tbsp chopped fresh parsley or 1 tsp chopped fresh coriander (cilantro)
2 tbsp soured cream or natural fromage frais (optional)
salt and pepper

OCEAN PIE:
175 g/6 oz white fish fillet, such as cod
4 tbsp milk
45 g/1½ oz/¼ cup peeled prawns (shrimp)
45 g/1½ oz/½ cup mushrooms, chopped roughly
½ tsp dried tarragon
250 g/8 oz/1 cup mashed potatoes
salt and pepper

1 Heat the oil in a saucepan and fry the onion and garlic gently until soft. Add the tomatoes, tomato purée (paste), water and seasoning. Bring to the boil. Cover and simmer gently for 10 minutes.

2 Cook the pasta in boiling salted water for about 10 minutes, or until just tender.

3 Heat the bacon gently in a saucepan until the fat runs, then add the mushrooms and continue cooking for 3–4 minutes. Drain off any excess oil and add half the tomato sauce with the parsley or coriander (cilantro), and the soured cream if using. Reheat and serve with the well-drained pasta. Set aside the remaining sauce.

4 To make the Ocean Pie, poach the fish in the milk with seasoning added until tender, about 6–8 minutes; then drain.

5 Heat the tomato sauce with the prawns (shrimp), mushrooms and tarragon. Flake the fish, discarding any skin and bones, and add to the sauce. Transfer to an ovenproof dish.

6 Pipe or spread the potatoes over the fish and place in a preheated oven at 200°C/400°F/Gas Mark 6 for about 25 minutes, or until golden brown.

STEP 1

STEP 3

STEP 5

STEP 6

STEP 1

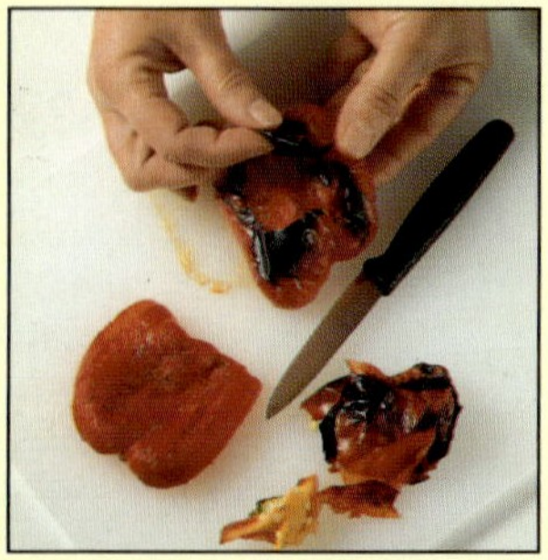

STEP 2

STEP 5

STEP 6

TABBOULEH SALAD

This kind of salad is eaten widely throughout the Middle East. Bulgar wheat is easy to prepare: simply soak it in boiling water before adding a variety of ingredients to make this unusual salad. The flavour improves as it is kept, so it tastes even better on the second day.

SERVES 2

125 g/4 oz/1 cup bulgar wheat
600 ml/1 pint/2½ cups boiling water
1 red (bell) pepper, halved
3 tbsp olive oil
1 garlic clove, crushed
grated rind of ½ lime
about 1 tbsp lime juice
1 tbsp chopped fresh mint
1 tbsp chopped fresh parsley
3–4 spring onions (scallions), trimmed and thinly sliced
8 pitted black olives, halved
45 g/1½ oz/⅓ cup large salted peanuts or cashew nuts
1–2 tsp lemon juice
60–90 g/2–3 oz Gruyère cheese
salt and pepper
fresh mint sprigs to garnish

1 Put the bulgar into a bowl and cover with the boiling water (it should come about 2.5 cm/1 inch above the bulgar). Leave to soak until most of the water has been absorbed and it is cold – up to an hour.

2 Meanwhile, put the halved red (bell) pepper, skin-side upwards, on a grill (broiler) rack and cook under a preheated moderate grill (broiler) until the skin is thoroughly charred. Leave to cool slightly, then peel off the skin and discard the seeds. Cut the (bell) pepper flesh into narrow strips.

3 Whisk together the oil, garlic, lime rind and juice, and seasoning until well blended. Add 1½ tablespoons of the dressing to the (bell) peppers and mix lightly.

4 Drain the soaked bulgar wheat thoroughly, squeezing it in a dry cloth to make it even drier, and place in a bowl.

5 Add the chopped herbs, spring onions (scallions), olives and peanuts or cashew nuts to the bulgar and toss thoroughly. Add the lemon juice to the remaining dressing, and stir through the salad. Spoon the salad on to one side of 2 serving plates.

6 Cut the cheese into narrow strips and mix with the (bell) pepper strips. Spoon alongside the bulgar salad. Garnish with mint sprigs and serve with warm pitta (pocket) bread or crusty rolls.

STEP 1

STEP 2

STEP 3

STEP 5

BOBOTIE/CREAMY CURRIED BEEF

Rich savoury minced (ground) beef is flavoured with spices, raisins, tomatoes and almonds; the next day the leftovers are transfomed into a delicious creamy curry.

SERVES 1

350 g/12 oz/1½ cups minced (ground) beef
1 onion, chopped
1 garlic clove, crushed
1 large carrot, chopped finely
2 tomatoes, peeled and sliced
2 tsp tomato purée (paste)
60 g/2 oz/⅓ cup raisins or sultanas (golden raisins)
150 ml/¼ pint/⅔ cup beef stock
1½ tbsp wine vinegar
½ tsp ground cumin
¼ tsp ground cinnamon
generous pinch of ground allspice
30 g/1 oz/¼ cup flaked (slivered) almonds
salt and pepper

CREAMY CURRIED BEEF:
1 tsp medium curry powder
60 g/2 oz/¼ cup long-grain rice
2–3 tbsp sour cream or natural yogurt

TO GARNISH:
1–2 tomatoes
½ small onion
2 poppadoms

1 Put the beef, onion, garlic and carrot into a saucepan and heat gently until the fat runs, then continue until the beef is well sealed.

2 Add the tomatoes, tomato purée (paste), raisins or sultanas (golden raisins), stock, vinegar, spices and seasoning, and bring to the boil. Cover and simmer gently for 20 minutes, until very tender, stirring occasionally.

3 Transfer half the mixture to a bowl and leave to cool, then chill. Add the flaked (slivered) almonds to the remaining beef in the saucepan, and adjust the seasoning. Cook for a further 2–3 minutes; then serve.

4 The next day, put the beef mixture into a small saucepan and reheat gently. Then add the curry powder and a little water if it seems too dry, and simmer for 10 minutes. At the same time, cook the rice in boiling salted water for about 12–14 minutes or until tender.

5 Stir the sour cream or yogurt into the beef and reheat gently. Drain the rice.

6 Slice the tomatoes thinly and the onion very thinly, and mix together. Arrange the rice in a ring on a warmed plate, spoon the curried beef into the centre and serve with the tomato and onion salad and poppadoms.

CHAPTER FOUR

Main Courses

A meal is usually planned around the main dish, so once you have made your choice, you can then select the vegetable accompaniments. Try to serve potatoes, pasta or rice with at least one other vegetable; the calorie-conscious can omit the potatoes and serve two vegetables, one of which should be green. If you are serving a starter and a dessert, it is important to choose foods that complement each other. Do not serve two dishes made with pastry, or two dishes which are fried; try to balance a slightly heavier main course with a lighter dessert and vice versa.

When you use the oven, it is economical to cook as much food in it at one time as you can. For instance, put a potato or two in to bake and then add the main dish for the required time. Several vegetables can be cooked together in the same saucepan; ideally you should use a pan with special partitions, but if you don't have one, start off with the vegetable that takes the longest to cook and then add the rest in turn, according to their cooking time. Drain them together when ready and serve topped with a knob of butter. If you feel that making a white sauce for just one vegetable portion is extravagant or time-wasting, simply top the vegetable with a tablespoon or two of fromage frais, natural yogurt or sour cream – not quite the same as a white sauce but still very good.

Opposite: *Choose a range of different meats and fish to add to your favourite vegetables to create a selection of hearty and satisfying main courses.*

STEP 1

STEP 2

STEP 4

STEP 5

SEAFISH BUNDLES

A mixture of white fish and shellfish in a tangy sauce baked in crisp filo pastry bundles.

SERVES 2

30 g/1 oz/2 tbsp peeled prawns (shrimp)
8 bottled mussels
175–250 g/6–8 oz white fish fillets (e.g. cod, haddock, plaice), skinned
45 g/1½ oz/½ cup button mushrooms
1–2 spring onions (scallions), trimmed
½ tsp chopped fresh dill or a large pinch dried dillweed
2 tbsp natural fromage frais
1 tbsp thick mayonnaise
6 sheets filo pastry
about 15 g/½ oz/1 tbsp butter or margarine, melted
salt and pepper

SAUCE:
4 tbsp natural fromage frais
2 tbsp thick mayonnaise
pinch of chopped fresh dill or dried dillweed

TO GARNISH:
cooked prawns (shrimp) in shells (optional)
fresh herbs
lime slices or wedges

1 Put the prawns (shrimp) into a bowl, halving if large, and then add the mussels. Cut the fish into small cubes; add to the prawns (shrimp).

2 Chop the mushrooms and slice the spring onion (scallion). Add to the fish with the herbs, fromage frais, mayonnaise and seasoning. Mix well.

3 Halve each sheet of filo pastry. Place 1 piece on a flat surface and brush lightly with the melted butter. Cover with another sheet at right angles to the first and brush again. Then add a third sheet and brush again. Repeat with 3 other piles of filo pastry.

4 Divide the fish mixture evenly between the bundles. Gather the corners of the pastry together carefully and press together to form a bundle.

5 Stand on a greased baking sheet and brush the pastry with melted fat. Place in a preheated oven at 190°C/375°F/Gas Mark 5 for about 25 minutes, or until golden brown and cooked.

6 While the bundles cook, make the sauce. Combine the fromage frais and mayonnaise in a saucepan and heat gently, but do not boil. Add the dill and seasoning to taste and serve with the bundles, garnished with prawns (shrimp) in their shells, fresh herbs and lime slices.

STEP 1

STEP 2

STEP 3

STEP 6

SCALLOP & BACON KEBAB

Just for one, this kebab will give a taste of elegance with very little preparation and cooking.

SERVES 1

2 large scallops or 6–8 queen scallops
6 lean streaky bacon rashers (slices), derinded
1 small courgette (zucchini), trimmed
1 tsp balsamic vinegar
1 tsp oil
1 tsp lemon juice
generous pinch of dried thyme
pepper

COCONUT RICE:
generous pinch of turmeric
pinch of salt
1 tbsp desiccated (shredded) coconut
60 g/2 oz/$^1/_4$ cup long-grain rice

TO GARNISH:
watercress
tomato slices

1 If using large scallops, cut each one into 3 pieces. Wrap a rasher (slice) of bacon around each piece or around each of the small scallops, if using.

2 Cut the courgette (zucchini) diagonally into 5 slices. Thread on to a long skewer, alternating with the scallop and bacon rolls.

3 Combine the vinegar, oil, lemon juice, thyme and pepper, and brush over the kebab. Leave on a plate while cooking the rice.

4 Bring a small saucepan of water to the boil with the turmeric and salt added. Add the coconut and rice and bring back to the boil. Simmer, uncovered, for 12–14 minutes until tender.

5 Place the kebabs under a preheated moderate grill (broiler) for 2–3 minutes on each side until the bacon is crispy and the scallop just cooked.

6 Drain the rice thoroughly and arrange on a warm serving plate. Place the kebab across the rice and garnish with watercress and tomato slices.

COQ AU VIN BLANC

Small pieces of chicken are gently simmered with wine, herbs, bacon, mushrooms and onions to produce a dish reminiscent of a true French meal.

SERVES 2

2 chicken leg quarters
90 g/3 oz/4 thick lean back bacon rashers (slices), derinded
2 tbsp oil
125 g/4 oz button onions or 1 large onion, sliced
1 garlic clove, crushed
150 ml/¼ pint/⅔ cup dry white wine
300 ml/½ pint/1¼ cups chicken stock
1 bay leaf
large pinch of dried oregano
1 tbsp cornflour (cornstarch)
60 g/2 oz/¾ cup tiny button mushrooms, trimmed
salt and pepper
chopped fresh parsley to garnish

1 Cut each chicken leg into 2 pieces and season well. Cut the bacon into 1 cm/½ inch strips.

2 Heat the oil in a saucepan. Fry the chicken until golden brown and remove from the pan. Add the bacon, onions and garlic, and fry until lightly browned. Drain off all the fat from the saucepan.

3 Add the wine, stock, bay leaf, oregano and seasoning to the saucepan, return the chicken and bring to the boil.

4 Cover the saucepan tightly and simmer very gently for about 40–50 minutes, or until the chicken is very tender.

5 Blend the cornflour (cornstarch) with a little cold water and add to the saucepan with the mushrooms. Bring back to the boil and simmer for a further 5 minutes.

6 Adjust the seasoning, discard the bay leaf and serve sprinkled liberally with chopped parsley, and with boiled rice or creamed potatoes.

VARIATION

For a traditional Coq au Vin, replace the white wine with red wine and add 1–2 tablespoons of brandy (if liked) after the cornflour (cornstarch).

STEP 1

STEP 2

STEP 3

STEP 5

STEP 1

STEP 2

STEP 3

STEP 4

PAN-FRIED LIVER WITH THYME AND CAPERS

This elegant dish is very simple to make. You can use either calf's or lamb's liver for the main ingredient.

SERVES 1

1 slice calf's liver, about 125 g/4 oz, or 2 smaller slices, or 2 slices lamb's liver
1 tbsp seasoned flour
2 tsp oil
15 g/½ oz/1 tbsp butter or margarine
2 tbsp white wine
½ tsp chopped fresh thyme or a large pinch of dried thyme
pinch of finely grated lime or lemon rind
2 tsp lemon juice
1 tsp capers
1–2 tbsp double (heavy) cream (optional)
salt and pepper

TO GARNISH:
lemon or lime slices
fresh thyme or parsley

1 Trim the liver if necessary and toss evenly in the seasoned flour.

2 Heat the oil and butter or margarine in a frying pan (skillet). When foaming, add the liver and fry for 2–3 minutes on each side until well sealed and just cooked through. Take care not to overcook or the liver will become tough and hard. Transfer to a plate and keep warm.

3 Add the wine, 1 tablespoon of water, the thyme, citrus rind, lemon juice, capers and seasoning to the pan juices, and heat through gently until bubbling and syrupy.

4 If liked, add the cream to the sauce and reheat gently. Adjust the seasoning and spoon over the liver.

5 Serve the liver, garnished with lemon or lime slices and thyme or parsley, with new potatoes and a salad.

GARNISH

Liver is traditionally served with bacon and onions, and grilled bacon rolls and crisply fried onions can be used as an extra garnish.

STEP 1

STEP 2

STEP 3

STEP 4

NOISETTES OF LAMB WITH SPICY SAUCE

Grilled (broiled) or fried noisettes of lamb are served on croûtes of fried bread or toast with a spicy tomato and mushroom sauce. Pork noisettes are equally tasty, if you prefer.

SERVES 2

4 lamb noisettes or cutlets or 4 pork noisettes or boneless pork slices
4 × 10 cm/4 inch rounds of bread
oil or fat for shallow-frying (optional)
fresh herbs to garnish

SAUCE:
6 tbsp red wine
6 tbsp tomato ketchup
2 tbsp water
1 garlic clove, crushed
60 g/2 oz/¾ cup button mushrooms, sliced or quartered
salt and pepper

1 To make the sauce, put the wine, tomato ketchup, water and garlic into a saucepan, bring to the boil and simmer, uncovered, for 10 minutes until beginning to thicken and evaporate a little. Add seasoning and the mushrooms, and cook for a further 10 minutes or so, or until the sauce is thick and syrupy and reduced by at least a third.

2 Meanwhile, prepare the noisettes. Place the meat on a piece of foil on a grill (broiler) rack and season lightly. If you cannot buy noisettes, bone out each lamb cutlet carefully and roll up with the eye of the meat in the centre, then secure with wooden cocktail sticks (toothpicks) or string.

3 Place the noisettes under a preheated moderate grill (broiler) for about 5 minutes on each side until browned and just cooked through; if you are using lamb, they can be left just slightly pink in the centre – do not overcook. Alternatively, they may be fried gently in the minimum of fat in a frying pan (skillet) for about 6–7 minutes on each side.

4 The rounds of bread may be fried quickly in a little heated oil for 1–2 minutes on each side, and then drained on paper towels. Otherwise simply toast the rounds on each side until golden brown.

5 Serve each noisette on a bread croûte and spoon the sauce over and around each one. Garnish with fresh herbs. Serve with lightly cooked fresh vegetables.

STEP 1

STEP 2

STEP 4

STEP 5

TURKISH LAMB STEW

A delicious blend of flavours with lamb, onions and tomatoes, complete with potatoes to make a one-pot dish for two, which just needs a salad accompaniment.

SERVES 2

350 g/12 oz lean boneless lamb
1 large or 2 small onions
1 garlic clove, crushed
½ red, yellow or green (bell) pepper, diced roughly
300 ml/½ pint/1¼ cups stock
1 tbsp balsamic vinegar
2 tomatoes, peeled and chopped roughly
1½ tsp tomato purée (paste)
1 bay leaf
½ tsp dried sage
½ tsp dried dillweed
350 g/12 oz potatoes
6–8 black olives, halved and pitted
salt and pepper

1 Cut the lamb into cubes about 2 cm/¾ inch, discarding any excess fat or gristle. Place in a non-stick saucepan with no extra fat and heat gently until the fat runs and the meat begins to seal.

2 Cut the onion into 8 wedges. Add to the lamb with the garlic and fry for a further 3–4 minutes.

3 Add the (bell) pepper, stock, vinegar, tomatoes, tomato purée (paste), bay leaf, sage, dillweed and seasoning. Cover and simmer gently for 30 minutes.

4 Peel the potatoes and cut into 2 cm/¾ inch cubes. Add to the stew and stir well. If necessary, add a little more boiling stock or water if it seems a little dry. Cover the pan again and simmer for a further 25–30 minutes, or until tender.

5 Add the olives and adjust the seasoning. Simmer for a further 5 minutes and serve with vegetables or a salad and crusty bread.

SALAD ACCOMPANIMENT

A good salad accompaniment would be shredded white cabbage, Little Gem lettuce, coarsely grated carrot, diced avocado or cucumber and spring onions (scallions).

CHAPTER FIVE

Desserts

Nearly everyone loves dessert, so don't be deterred from making them for only one or two people. It is probably better to make enough for two people, even if you are on your own – somehow an extra dessert is always a welcome leftover in the fridge, and it saves time the next day or the day after. Many desserts will keep for two or three days, so serve something different on the intervening day.

Whether you are making a dessert just for yourself or are planning a special meal for two, the ideas in this chapter cover hot and cold desserts and use a wide range of flavours and ingredients. White chocolate is becoming as popular as its dark and milk counterparts and gives a new dimension to chocolate mousse; syllabub is an old favourite, but here has a subtle flavour and the colour of blackcurrants from the liqueur; Alaskas, although traditionally made with ice cream in the centre and masked in meringue, can instead be assembled with a delicious filling of fruits on the ginger cake base; lime and mint give a splendid flavour and pretty speckled appearance to the cheesecakes with a chocolate base; a can of rice pudding, bananas and brown sugar are store cupboard items ideal for an almost instant dessert; and pancakes filled and shaped into bundles with a raspberry sauce show you another delicious way of serving pancakes.

Opposite: *A dessert can consist of just fresh fruit, simply prepared. The advantage of cooking for one or two people is that using small quantities of expensive or exotic fruits is more affordable than if you are cooking for a crowd.*

STEP 2

STEP 3

STEP 5

STEP 6

LIME CHEESECAKES

These cheesecakes are flavoured with lime and mint, and set on a base of crushed biscuits (crackers) mixed with chocolate.

SERVES 2

BASE:
30 g/1 oz/2 tbsp butter
30 g/1 oz/1 square dark chocolate
90 g/3 oz/¾ cup digestive biscuits (graham crackers), crushed

FILLING:
finely grated rind of 1 lime
90 g/3 oz/⅓ cup curd (creamed cottage) cheese
90 g/3 oz/⅓ cup low-fat soft cheese
1 sprig fresh mint, chopped very finely (optional)
1 tsp powdered gelatine
1 tbsp lime juice
1 egg yolk
45 g/1½ oz/3 tbsp caster (superfine) sugar

TO DECORATE:
whipped cream
kiwi fruit slices
fresh mint sprigs

1 Grease 2 fluted, preferably loose-bottomed 11 cm/4½ inch flan tins (pans) thoroughly. To make the base, melt the butter and chocolate in a heatproof bowl over a pan of gently simmering water, or melt in a microwave set on Full Power for about 1 minute. Stir until smooth.

2 Stir the crushed biscuits evenly through the melted chocolate and then press into the bases of the flan tins (pans), levelling the top. Chill until set.

3 To make the filling, put the grated lime rind and cheeses into a bowl and beat until smooth and evenly blended, then beat in the mint, if using.

4 Dissolve the gelatine in the lime juice in a heatproof bowl over a saucepan of gently simmering water, or in a microwave oven set on Full Power for about 30 seconds.

5 Beat the egg yolk and sugar together until thick and creamy and fold through the cheese mixture, followed by the dissolved gelatine. Pour over the set biscuit base and level the top, if necessary; then chill until set.

6 To serve, remove the cheesecakes carefully from the flan tins (pans) and ease off the metal bases, if necessary. Decorate with whipped cream, slices of kiwi fruit and mint sprigs.

STEP 2

STEP 3

STEP 5

STEP 6

GINGER & APRICOT ALASKAS

No ice cream in this Alaska but a mixture of apples and apricots poached in orange juice enclosed in meringue.

SERVES 2

2 slices rich, dark ginger cake, about 2 cm/$^3/_4$ inch thick
1–2 tbsp ginger wine or rum
1 dessert (eating) apple
6 no-need-to-soak dried apricots, chopped
4 tbsp orange juice or water
15 g/$^1/_2$ oz/1 tbsp flaked (slivered) almonds
2 small egg whites
100 g/3$^1/_2$ oz/$^1/_3$ cup caster (superfine) sugar

1 Place each slice of ginger cake on an ovenproof plate and sprinkle with the ginger wine or rum.

2 Quarter, core and slice the apple into a small saucepan. Add the chopped apricots and orange juice or water, and simmer gently for about 5 minutes, or until tender.

3 Stir the almonds into the fruit and spoon over the soaked cake, piling it up in the centre.

4 Whisk the egg whites until very stiff and dry, then whisk in the sugar a little at a time, making sure the meringue is stiff again before adding more sugar.

5 Either pipe or spread the meringue over the fruit and cake, making sure it is completely covered.

6 Place in a preheated oven at 200°C/400°F/Gas Mark 6 for 4–5 minutes until golden brown. Serve hot.

VARIATION

A slice of vanilla, coffee or chocolate ice cream can be placed on the fruit before adding the meringue, but this must be done at the last minute and the dessert must be eaten immediately after it is removed from the oven.

STEP 2

STEP 3

STEP 4

STEP 5

RASPBERRY & ORANGE PANCAKE BUNDLES

This unusual pancake is filled with a sweet cream flavoured with ginger, nuts and apricots and served with a raspberry and orange sauce. The surplus batter will keep in the refrigerator for a few days.

SERVES 2

BATTER:
60 g/2 oz/$^1/_2$ cup plain (all-purpose) flour
pinch of salt
$^1/_4$ tsp ground cinnamon
1 egg
135 ml/4$^1/_2$ fl oz/generous $^1/_2$ cup milk
white vegetable fat for frying

FILLING:
1$^1/_2$ tsp plain (all-purpose) flour, sifted
1$^1/_2$ tsp cornflour (cornstarch)
1 tbsp caster (superfine) sugar
1 egg
150 ml/$^1/_4$ pint/$^2/_3$ cup milk
30 g/1 oz/$^1/_4$ cup chopped nuts
45 g/1$^1/_2$ oz/$^1/_4$ cup no-need-to-soak dried apricots, chopped
1 piece stem (candied) or crystallized ginger, finely chopped

SAUCE:
3 tbsp raspberry preserve
1$^1/_2$ tbsp orange juice
finely grated rind of $^1/_4$ orange

1 To make the batter, sift the flour, salt and cinnamon into a bowl and make a well in the centre. Add the egg and beat in the flour and milk gradually until smooth.

2 Melt a small knob of the fat in a medium frying pan (skillet). When hot, pour in enough batter to cover the base thinly. Cook for 2 minutes until golden brown, then cook the other side until browned, about 1 minute. Set aside and make a second pancake.

3 For the filling, beat together the flour, cornflour (cornstarch), sugar and egg. Heat the milk gently in a pan, then beat 2 tablespoons of it into the flour mixture. Transfer to the saucepan and cook gently, stirring continuously until thick. Remove from the heat, cover with baking parchment to prevent a skin forming and leave to cool.

4 Beat the nuts, apricots and ginger into the cooled mixture and put a heaped tablespoonful in the centre of each pancake. Gather and squeeze the edges together to make a bundle. Place in an ovenproof dish in a preheated oven at 180°C/350°F/Gas Mark 4 for 15–20 minutes until hot but not too brown.

5 To make the sauce, melt the preserve gently with the orange juice, then sieve (strain). Return to a clean pan with the orange rind and heat through. Serve with the pancakes.

PINK SYLLABUBS

The pretty pink colour of this dessert is achieved by adding blackcurrant liqueur to the wine and cream before whipping.

SERVES 2

5 tbsp white wine
2–3 tsp blackcurrant liqueur
finely grated rind of ½ lemon or orange
1 tbsp caster (superfine) sugar
200 ml/7 fl oz/scant 1 cup double (heavy) cream
4 boudoir biscuits (lady-fingers) (optional)

TO DECORATE:
fresh fruit, such as strawberries, raspberries or redcurrants, or pecan or walnut halves
fresh mint sprigs

1 Mix together the white wine, blackcurrant liqueur, grated lemon or orange rind and caster (superfine) sugar in a bowl and leave for at least 30 minutes.

2 Add the double (heavy) cream to the wine mixture and whip until the mixture thickens enough to stand in soft peaks.

3 If you are using the boudoir biscuits (lady-fingers), break them up roughly and divide them between 2 glasses.

4 Put the mixture into a piping bag fitted with a large star or plain nozzle (tip) and pipe it over the biscuits (lady-fingers). Alternatively, simply pour the syllabub over the biscuits (lady-fingers). Chill until ready to serve.

5 Before serving, decorate each syllabub with slices or small pieces of fresh soft fruit or nuts, and sprigs of mint.

NOTE

These syllabubs will keep in the refrigerator for 48 hours, so it is worth making more than you need, and keeping the extra for another day.

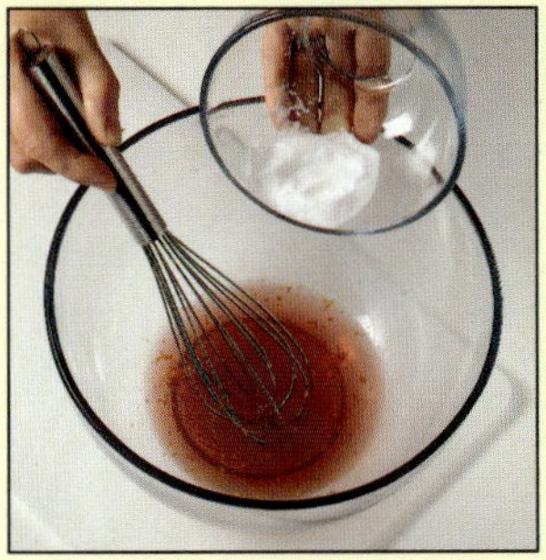
STEP 1

STEP 2

STEP 3

STEP 4

STEP 1

STEP 3

STEP 4

STEP 5

RICE AND BANANA BRULEE

Take a can of rice pudding, flavour it with orange rind, stem (candied) ginger, raisins and sliced bananas and top with a brown sugar glaze for a real treat.

SERVES 2

425 g/15 oz can of creamed rice pudding
grated rind of ½ orange
2 pieces stem (candied) ginger, chopped finely
2 tsp ginger syrup from the jar
45 g/1½ oz/¼ cup raisins
1–2 bananas
1–2 tsp lemon juice
4–5 tbsp demerara (brown crystal) sugar

1 Empty the can of rice pudding into a bowl and mix in the grated orange rind, ginger, ginger syrup and raisins.

2 Cut the bananas diagonally into slices, toss in the lemon juice, drain and divide between 2 individual flameproof dishes.

3 Spoon the rice mixture in an even layer over the bananas so the dishes are almost full.

4 Sprinkle an even layer of sugar over the rice in each dish.

5 Place the dishes under a preheated moderate grill (broiler) and heat until the sugar melts, taking care the sugar does not burn.

6 Leave to cool until the caramel sets, then chill until ready to serve. Tap the caramel with the back of a spoon to break it.

CANNED RICE PUDDING

Canned rice pudding is very versatile and is delicious heated with orange segments and grated apples added. Try it served cold with grated chocolate and mixed chopped nuts stirred through it.

STEP 1

STEP 2

STEP 3

STEP 4

WHITE CHOCOLATE POTS

A delicious white chocolate and rum mousse, which is only softly set and flavoured with fromage frais.

SERVES 2

90 g/3 oz/3 squares white chocolate
15 g/½ oz/1 tbsp butter
1 tbsp rum
1 egg, separated
1 tbsp natural fromage frais

TO DECORATE:
whipped cream or natural fromage frais
fresh raspberries (optional)
fresh mint leaves

1 Break up the white chocolate and put into a heatproof bowl with the butter. Place over a saucepan of very gently simmering water, and heat gently until completely melted, stirring frequently.

2 Remove the bowl from the heat and beat in the rum, followed by the egg yolk and finally the fromage frais. Leave to cool.

3 Whisk the egg white until very stiff and dry, and fold evenly through the white chocolate mixture.

4 Divide between 2 individual serving pots and chill until set. This mousse does not set very firmly.

5 Before serving, top each pot with a spoonful of whipped cream or fromage frais and decorate with a few raspberries and fresh mint leaves. Alternatively, sprinkle with some grated dark chocolate, or a chocolate flake bar, roughly crumbled.

VARIATION

For a variation, 1–2 tablespoons of coarsely grated chocolate can be folded through the mixture with the egg white or dark chocolate may be used instead of white chocolate. The grated rind of ½ small orange may also be added to give an orange flavouring.

MEALS FOR ONE & TWO

CAKES
A piece of cake can bridge the gap between lunch and dinner, or serve as a dessert to any meal, so it is worth always having a cake in the cupboard. Here are a few ideas:

Madeira Loaf (Pound Cake)
125 g/4 oz /1 cup self-raising flour
60 g/2 oz/1/2 cup plain (all-purpose) flour
125 g/4 oz/1/2 cup butter
125 g/4 oz/1/2 cup caster (superfine) sugar
finely grated rind of 1 lemon
2 eggs
1 tbsp lemon juice

1. Grease and line a loaf tin (pan), approx 23 × 12.5 cm/ 9 × 5 inches, with greased greaseproof paper or non-stick baking parchment.

2. Sift the flours together. Cream the fat and sugar together until very light and fluffy and pale in colour.

3. Beat in the lemon rind, then the eggs, adding a tablespoon of flour after each egg.

4. Fold the flours into the mixture followed by sufficient lemon juice to give a dropping consistency.

5. Turn the mixture into the tin (pan) and level the top. Bake in a preheated oven at 160°C/ 325°F/Gas Mark 3 for about 1 hour, until well risen and firm.

Whatever your situation, whether you are young or old, living alone or in a couple, retired or working full time, cooking for just one or two can present a problem. Either there is no time for shopping or elaborate cooking; or you have plenty of time, but not the inclination to make the effort to prepare a lunch or supper just for one. So, like many people, you need a number of quick and simple recipes that don't need elaborate ingredients, nor require you to spend hours in the kitchen, and which are interesting as well as nutritious. The important factor is to keep the meals well balanced for a healthy diet. The recipes in this book will help you to do this, and show that you don't have to resort to junk food for convenience, or live on tinned and pre-cooked food. It will also show you that it is not too much trouble to cook for just one or two people, particularly when meals can be made to stretch over two days, or even be reworked into a different dish, to serve up the following day,

BREAKFASTS
A normal breakfast for one or two will probably be based upon a bowl of cereal, followed by buttered toast perhaps spread with jam, with tea or coffee to drink. Making your breakfasts more varied doesn't have to mean a dramatic increase in preparation time, but it can make your breakfast much more interesting, and can increase the nutritional value.

Try adding or substituting one or more of the following items to your normal breakfast, or perhaps just at weekends.

- A glass of fruit juice – orange, grapefruit, pineapple, tomato; if you have the equipment, these are best when freshly squeezed. Not only do they taste better, but they also contain more vitamins.
- A bowl of homemade muesli with added fresh fruit, grated or sliced
- Sliced bananas, apples or soft fruit added to your normal cereal and topped with natural yogurt or fromage frais
- Croissants or muffins, warmed in the oven, with jam or honey
- Scrambled egg: use 2 eggs per person and, if you like, add 30 g/1 oz chopped smoked salmon pieces
- Smoked haddock kedgeree (see below)
- Poached smoked haddock, with a poached egg on top if you like
- Poached or grilled kippers
- Grilled bacon with sausages and/or tomatoes and mushrooms
- Pancakes with maple syrup
- Spanish Omelette (see below)
- Boiled eggs

Spanish Omelette
Serves 1
2–3 rashers (slices) bacon, rinded
1 small onion, finely chopped
1–2 tbsp oil
1 large boiled potato, diced
30 g/1 oz/1/3 cup mushrooms, sliced, and/or 1–2 tomatoes, peeled and sliced

2–3 eggs
1 tbsp water
salt and pepper

1. Chop the bacon and fry the bacon and onion in the heated oil in a frying pan (skillet) until sealed and lightly browned.

2. Add the potato and mushrooms and/or tomatoes and continue cooking for 1–2 minutes.

3. Beat the eggs with the water and seasonings, pour into the frying pan (skillet), mix lightly, then leave to settle. Cook over a gentle heat until set. If liked, place under a preheated moderate grill (broiler) to brown the top. Serve hot.

Smoked Haddock Kedgeree
Make as for Salmon Kedgeree on page 36, but poach 175–250 g/6–8 oz smoked haddock fillet in a little water or milk and water mixed until tender, about 5 minutes; then drain, remove skin and bones and flake roughly.

LIGHT LUNCHES AND PACKED LUNCHES

There are always days when a quick light lunch is required, or you need to pack up something to take to work or for a trip of some sort. Often these snacks will be simple and comprise sandwiches or rolls with various fillings, sometimes incorporating bought ingredients such as pâté, cheese, tinned fish and so on. The main problem is making sure that such a meal, however small, is properly balanced, filling enough and easy to carry if it is to be taken with you.

Salads
Salads are simple, can easily be prepared using a wide range of fresh ingredients plus a dressing if wanted and packed into an empty margarine carton if you are eating on the move. Rolls, bread or crackers make a good accompaniment together with a fruit or natural yogurt or some fromage frais and/or a piece of fruit together with a soft drink carton or can. Another salad snack that is quick to prepare is a plate of crudités eaten with a dip such as hummus or taramasalata. If teamed with a slice or two of wholemeal (whole wheat) bread, this makes a nutritious snack.

Sandwiches
If you want to make sandwiches or filled rolls, then try a variety of fillings.

- Mix a can of tuna with a touch of mayonnaise, chopped onion, lettuce and tomato.
- On the next day, the tuna can be flavoured with sweetcorn or chopped tomatoes, with a touch of French dressing and tomato ketchup, topped with sliced cucumber and/or cress.
- Leftover cold meats, such as roast beef or lamb, or pre-packed cold meats such as honey-roast ham or wafer-thin turkey make good fillings.
- Eggs can be used in numerous combinations, such as mixed with mayonnaise with horseradish, cress, curry powder and mango chutney, or grated cheese and tomato ketchup.
- Cheese can have unlimited accompaniments. Keep a selection of cheeses in the refrigerator to ensure a variety of flavours.

Coffee Sandwich Cake
125 g/4 oz/½ cup butter
125 g/4 oz/½ cup caster (superfine) sugar
2 eggs
125 g/4 oz/1 cup self-raising flour, sifted
3 tsp coffee flavouring (extract) or very strong black coffee

Butter Cream
60 g/2 oz/1 tbsp butter
125 g/4 oz/1 cup icing (confectioners') sugar, sifted
1 tsp coffee flavouring (extract) or very strong black coffee

1. Grease and base line 2 round 18 cm/7 inch sandwich tins (layer pans) with greased greaseproof paper or non-stick baking parchment.

2. Cream the fat and sugar together until very light and fluffy and pale in colour. Beat in the eggs, following each with a spoonful of the flour, and then fold in the remainder followed by the coffee.

3. Divide the mixture between the tins (pans), level the tops and bake in a preheated oven at 190°C/375°F/Gas Mark 5 for about 20 minutes or until well risen and firm.

4. Cool in the tins for a minute or so, then loosen the cakes, turn out on to a wire rack and leave until cold.

5. For the butter cream, soften the butter, then add sufficient

icing (confectioners') sugar and coffee flavouring (extract) to give a thick spreading consistency. Use to sandwich the cakes together and dredge the top lightly with sifted icing (confectioners') sugar.

Brownies

Makes 9–10

60 g/2 oz/2 squares dark chocolate
60 g/2 oz/1 tbsp butter
few drops of vanilla flavouring (extract)
175 g/6 oz caster (superfine) sugar
2 eggs
75 g/2½ oz/generous ½ cup self-raising flour, sifted
45 g/1½ oz/¼ cup chopped nuts or raisins

1. Grease and line a shallow 20 cm/8 inch square tin (pan) with greased greaseproof paper or baking parchment.

2. Melt the chocolate and the fat in a heatproof bowl, either over a saucepan of gently simmering water or in a microwave oven set on Full Power for 30–60 seconds.

3. Beat in the flavouring (extract) and sugar followed by the eggs. Fold in the flour, followed by the nuts or raisins and pour into the tin (pan).

4. Bake in a preheated oven at 180°C/350°F/Gas Mark 4 for about 30 minutes or until risen and firm. Cool in the tin (pan).

Wrap sandwiches or rolls in clingfilm (plastic wrap) or foil. If you have a sweet tooth then add a piece of cake or a couple of biscuits (cookies).

TEATIME

Teatime is popular with everyone and baking is an important part of everyday cooking, but when you are catering for one or two it is better to make small cakes and smaller batches, and perhaps choose those items that will keep well for several days or longer, rather than making those which are best eaten immediately.

For the recipes below, if you have a fan oven, it will be a little hotter than the conventional gas or electric oven, so lower the suggested temperature by about 10°C/25°F, and check the cake a few minutes before the end of the suggested cooking time.

Once made, all cakes should be cooled thoroughly and then stored in an airtight container. Empty margarine, yogurt and fromage frais containers are good for storing small buns and cakes; otherwise it is wise to buy a set of plastic containers which will cope with all shapes and sizes. When not in use they are can be stored one inside the other.

Here are a couple of teatime recipes; for more ideas, see the recipe columns either side of the pages in this section.

Scones

Makes 8

250 g/8 oz/2 cups self-raising flour
pinch of salt
1½ tbsp caster (superfine) sugar
60 g/2 oz/1 tbsp butter or margarine
1 egg, beaten
about 5 tbsp milk
1 tsp lemon juice
45 g/1½ oz sultanas (golden raisins) (optional)

1. Sift the flour and salt into a bowl and mix in the sugar. Rub in the fat until the mixture resembles fine breadcrumbs, then add the egg.

2. Combine the milk and lemon juice and add sufficient to form a fairly soft dough. Stir in the sultanas if using.

3. Turn out on to a lightly floured work surface (counter) and level to a rectangle about 2.5 cm/1 inch thick and 10 cm/4 inches wide. Cut into 8 squares.

4. Stand on a lightly floured baking (cookie) sheet and bake in a preheated oven at 220°C/ 425°F/Gas Mark 7 for 10–15 minutes until well risen and a light golden brown. Cool on a wire rack.

Flapjacks

Makes 9–10

125 g/4 oz/½ cup margarine
60 g/2 oz/½ cup caster (superfine) or light soft brown sugar
6 tbsp golden (light corn) syrup
250 g/8 oz/⅔ cup rolled oats

1. Grease or grease and line a 20 cm/8 inch shallow square cake tin (pan) with greased greaseproof paper or non-stick baking parchment.

2. Cream the fat and sugar until light and fluffy.

3. Heat the syrup until runny and beat it into the creamed mixture followed by the oats. Mix the ingredients thoroughly and spoon into the prepared tin (pan), pressing the mixture down well with the back of a spoon, especially into thc corners.

4. Bake in a preheated oven at 190°C/375°F/Gas Mark 5 for about 30–40 minutes or until firm and golden brown.

5. Leave in the tin (pan) until quite cold before removing from the tin (pan) and breaking or cutting into squares or bars.

SUPPERS

Provided you have eaten one good meal each day, it is quite acceptable to have a snack for the other main meal. Whether you are on your own or cooking for two, it is probably a good idea to vary when you eat this snack meal. For instance when there is something good to watch on the television, an early TV snack supper is ideal. When you have been out for a nice lunch, or if there are just two of you wanting a late supper in front of the fire, then that too is a good time for a snack supper.

Omelettes, scrambled eggs with bacon and tomatoes or mushrooms, poached eggs on toast with baked beans, or one of the recipes from the 'Snacks and Quick Meals' chapter will all fit the bill.

Homemade soup makes an excellent supper, particularly in the winter months, with perhaps just a good tasty cheese or two and bread or crackers, accompanied by a few grapes or sticks of celery. You can make a big pot of lentil or bean soup with vegetables thrown in, which will last for two or three days. Here is my recipe for a simple lentil soup.

Lentil Soup

Makes 2 generous portions
175 g/6 oz/1 cup red lentils
1.2 litres/2 pints/5 cups stock or water
1 onion, peeled or chopped
1 clove garlic, crushed
2 carrots, peeled and chopped
1–2 sticks celery, chopped
2 tomatoes, peeled and chopped
1 bay leaf
2 potatoes, peeled and diced
salt and pepper
1 tbsp wine vinegar

TO GARNISH:
chopped parsley
croûtons

1. Wash the lentils, then place in a saucepan with the stock.

2. Add the onion, garlic, carrot, celery, tomatoes, bay leaf and seasonings. Bring to the boil, cover and simmer gently for an hour or until the lentils are tender.

3. Add the potatoes and cook for about 20 minutes more, or until tender.

4. Remove the bay leaf and blend or sieve (strain) the soup and return to the pan. Adjust the seasoning, add the wine vinegar and reheat.

5. Serve in warmed bowls sprinkled with the chopped parsley and some fried croûtons.

Rock Buns

Makes 10–12
175 g/6 oz/1½ cups self-raising flour
½ tsp mixed spice
½ tsp ground cinnamon
90 g/3 oz/1½ tbsp butter
grated rind of 1 orange or lemon
90 g/3 oz/½ cup raisins
45 g/1½ oz/4½ tbsp cut mixed (candied) peel
1-2 pieces stem ginger, chopped (optional)
1 egg, beaten
about 1 tbsp milk

1. Grease 1 large or 2 smaller baking (cookie) sheets, or 10–12 patty tins (muffin pans).

2. Sift the flour and spices into a bowl, add the fat and rub in until the mixture resembles fine breadcrumbs.

3. Add the fruit rind, raisins, peel and ginger, if using, and mix well.

4. Add the egg and sufficient milk to mix to a stiff consistency. Put the mixture in 10–12 heaps on the baking (cookie) sheet or divide between the patty tins (muffin pans). Do not smooth the mixture.

5. Bake in a preheated oven at 200°C/400°F/Gas Mark 6 for about 20 minutes or until lightly browned and firm. Cool on a wire rack.

INDEX

Almonds: chicken and almond rissoles with stir-fried vegetables, 27
apples: ginger and apricot Alaskas, 66
apricots: ginger and apricot Alaskas, 66
aubergine (eggplant) with risotto stuffing, 30
avocados: salmon with avocado and tarragon sauce, 36
smoked salmon pâté with avocado, 12

Bacon:
courgette (zucchini), tarragon and bacon quiches, 22
Italian tomato sauce with pasta, 43
scallop and bacon kebab, 52
banana and rice brûlée, 72
beef:
bobotie, 46
creamy curried beef, 46
blackcurrant liqueur: pink syllabubs, 71
bobotie, 46
breakfasts, 76
broccoli with fluffy eggs, 32
brownies, 78
bulgar wheat: tabbouleh salad, 44
buns, rock, 78-9
butter cream, 77

Cakes:
brownies, 78
coffee sandwich cake, 77-8
flapjacks, 78-9
Madeira loaf (pound cake), 76
rock buns, 79
capers, pan-fried liver with thyme and, 56
caramel: rice and banana brûlée, 72
cheese:
peppered Camembert and nectarine salad, 14
walnut, egg and cheese pâté, 16
cheesecakes, lime, 64
chicken:
chicken and almond rissoles with stir-fried vegetables, 27
chicken and sweetcorn chowder, 8
coq au vin blanc, 54
crunchy-topped chicken, 40
pasta medley, 38
spiced chicken salad, 40
chocolate:
brownies, 78
white chocolate pots, 74
chowder, chicken and sweetcorn, 8
coconut rice, 52
coffee sandwich cake, 77-8
coq au vin blanc, 54
courgette (zucchini), tarragon and bacon quiches, 22
cream: pink syllabubs, 71
curried beef, creamy, 46

Decorations: spring onion (scallion) tassels, 20
desserts, 63-74

Eggplant see aubergine
eggs:
broccoli with fluffy eggs, 32
Spanish omelette, 76-7
walnut, egg and cheese pâté, 16

Filo pastry:
seafish bundles, 50
spinach filo baskets, 20
fish:
ocean pie, 43
seafish bundles, 50
flapjacks, 79
fritters, sweetcorn and potato, 24

Ginger and apricot Alaskas, 66
grapes:
pasta medley, 38
spiced chicken salad, 40

Italian tomato sauce with pasta, 43

Kebab, scallop and bacon, 52
kedgeree, 36
smoked haddock, 77

Lamb:
noisettes of lamb with spicy sauce, 58
Turkish lamb stew, 60
leek, potato and carrot soup, 10
lime cheesecakes, 64
liver: pan-fried liver with thyme and capers, 56
lunches, 77

Macaroni and tuna fish layer, 28
Madeira loaf (pound cake), 76
meringues: ginger and apricot Alaskas, 66
mousses: white chocolate pots, 74
mushrooms: Spanish omelette, 76-7
mussels: seafish bundles, 50

Nectarines: peppered Camembert and nectarine salad, 14

Oats: flapjacks, 78-9
ocean pie, 43
omelette, Spanish, 76-7
oranges: raspberry and orange pancake bundles, 68

Packed lunches, 77
pancake bundles, raspberry and orange, 68
pasta:
Italian tomato sauce with pasta, 43
pasta medley, 38
pâtés:
smoked salmon with avocado, 12
walnut, egg and cheese, 16
peppered Camembert and nectarine salad, 14
pink syllabubs, 71
pork: pasta medley, 38
potatoes:
leek, potato and carrot soup, 10
ocean pie, 43
Spanish omelette, 76-7
sweetcorn and potato fritters, 24
Turkish lamb stew, 60
pound cake see Madeira loaf
prawns (shrimp):
ocean pie, 43
seafish bundles, 50

Quiches, courgette (zucchini), tarragon and bacon, 22

Raspberry and orange pancake bundles, 68
rice:
aubergine (eggplant) with risotto stuffing, 30
coconut rice, 52
creamy curried beef, 46
kedgeree, 36
rice and banana brûlée, 72
smoked haddock kedgeree, 77
spiced chicken salad, 40
rice pudding, canned, 72
rissoles, chicken and almond, 27
rock buns, 79

Salads, 77
peppered Camembert and nectarine, 14
spiced chicken, 40
tabbouleh, 44
salmon:
kedgeree, 36
salmon with avocado and tarragon sauce, 36
sandwiches, 77-8
scallions see spring onions
scallop and bacon kebab, 52
scones, 78
seafish bundles, 50
smoked haddock kedgeree, 77
smoked salmon pâté with avocado, 12
soups:
chicken and sweetcorn chowder, 8
leek, potato and carrot soup, 10
Spanish omelette, 76
spinach filo baskets, 20
spring onion (scallion) tassels, 20
starters, 12-16
stew, Turkish lamb, 60
suppers, 78
sweetcorn:
chicken and sweetcorn chowder, 8
sweetcorn and potato fritters, 24
syllabubs, pink, 71

Tabbouleh salad, 44
teatime, 78-9
tomatoes:
Italian tomato sauce with pasta, 43
noisettes of lamb with spicy sauce, 58
tuna: macaroni and tuna fish layer, 28
Turkish lamb stew, 60

Vegetables, chicken and almond rissoles with stir-fried, 27

Walnut, egg and cheese pâté, 16
wine:
coq au vin blanc, 54
pink syllabubs, 71

Zucchini see courgettes